RIDING

RIDING

by Christine Keir
Illustrated by Glenn Steward

GRANADA
London Toronto Sydney New York

Granada Publishing Limited
Frogmore, St Albans, Herts AL2 2NF
and
36 Golden Square, London W1R 4AH
515 Madison Avenue, New York, NY 10022, USA
117 York Street, Sydney, NSW 2000, Australia
60 International Blvd, Rexdale, Ontario R9W 6J2, Canada
61 Beach Road, Auckland, New Zealand

Published by Granada Publishing 1983

British Library Cataloguing in Publication Data

Keir, Christine
Riding. – (Granada guides; 37)
1. Horsemanship – Juvenile literature
I. Title
798.2′3   SF309.2

ISBN 0 246 11981 0

Printed and bound in Great Britain by
William Collins Sons & Co Ltd, Glasgow

Contents

Riding Through the Ages

Sixty million years ago the earliest ancestor of the horse, known as Eohippus, existed. Hardly larger than a hare, it had toes. By around a million years ago a stocky, bristly-maned pony, referred to as Equus, had appeared, an animal which had four hooves, for the toes had disappeared. Bones of horses have been found in Stone Age caves dating from between 25,000 and 10,000 BC, positive proof that horses were then a source of food. Drawings in caves tell us that these early horses were distinctly pony-like.

Later, horses became part of Greek mythology. The winged horse Pegasus, the most famous, was believed to be the offspring of the sea-god Poseidon and the monster Medusa. After catching him with a golden bridle, Bellerophon tried to soar on his back up to Olympus, the home of the gods, only to be thrown down to the ground and blinded.

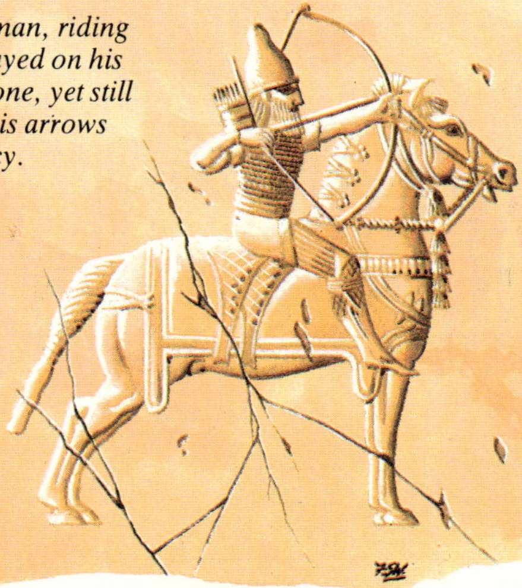

An Assyrian huntsman, riding without stirrups, stayed on his pony by balance alone, yet still managed to shoot his arrows with deadly accuracy.

Horses played an important part in Ancient Greek life. The winged horse Pegasus (right) was renowned in mythology, while bareback riders were skilfully carved into a famous frieze from the Parthenon in Athens (below).

Probably the first real evidence of riding is to be seen in the tomb of Horemheb, ruler of Egypt around 1400 BC, where the riders are depicted sitting on their horses' rumps without stirrups. By 890 BC the Assyrians were sitting farther forward and hunting lions as they rode. In the 4th century BC Xenophon, a Greek historian, wrote books on horsemanship, and much of what he wrote all those years ago is still valid today. The most famed Greek rider of those times was undoubtedly Alexander the Great, who rode his horse Bucephalus through many a campaign until his death in 323 BC.

It was the Huns who brought the stirrup to Europe in the 4th century AD. Mounted on Mongol ponies, they stood in their stirrups and rode with snaffle bits and loose reins.

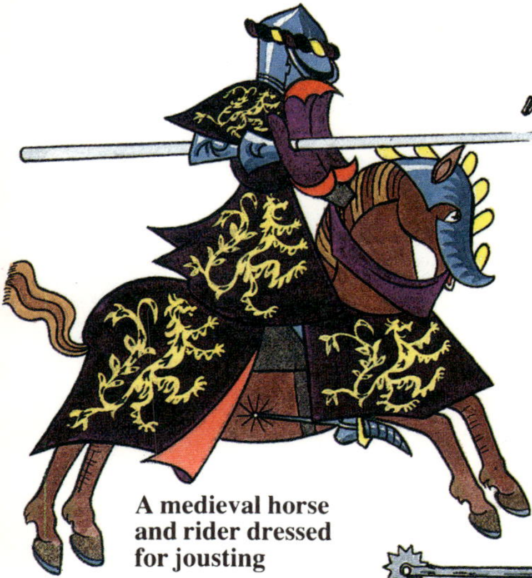

A medieval horse and rider dressed for jousting

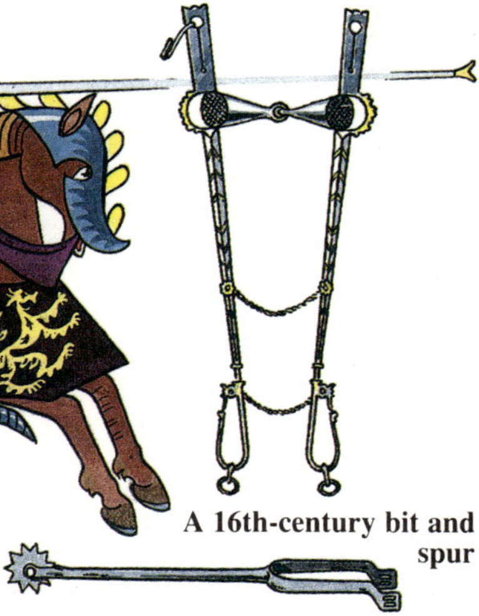

A 16th-century bit and spur

Knights in Shining Armour

Throughout the Middle Ages mounted warriors dominated the battlefield. Soon they were wearing armour, for this was a time of crusades and knighthood. At first they protected themselves with light chain-mail and rode small Arab-like horses, but as bowmen became more skilled, the armour became heavier to protect both horse and rider against the deadly arrows. Horses were bred larger to carry the enormous weight, and the knights themselves had to be lifted on to their backs by crane. In battle the knights held their reins and shields in their left hand, and their swords or lances in their right. Because of this they needed severe bits and long, sharp spurs to control the horses. When not fighting, knights held jousting contests and were so heavy in their armour that, once unseated, they were at the mercy of their opponents. Their huge horses came to be called Great Horses, the forebears of heavy horses today.

The Great Riding Schools

The 15th and 16th centuries saw the first riding schools. The School of Naples laid down the first rules of equitation, or horsemanship, and the School of Versailles was established in France in the reign of Louis XIV. It was during this time that the Duke of Newcastle's book *New Method of Horse Schooling* was published, but it was François de la Guérinière who was to become the greatest master of equitation in the 18th century. The famous cavalry school of Saumur in France was founded in 1771, but undoubtedly the celebrated Spanish Riding School in Vienna remains the best known today. Founded some 400 years ago, it has been the mecca of 'high school' ever since. Its famous Lipizzaner stallions undergo long and arduous training and their glittering displays are justly renowned.

Riding at its most superb as horses perform the Quadrille at the celebrated Spanish Riding School in Vienna.

Horses in War and Peace

The Huns, the Mongols and the Cossacks were all renowned riders in war, but surely the most famous, and saddest, cavalry charge of all was made by the British Light Brigade at Balaclava, Russia, in 1855, a catastrophe immortalized by the poet Tennyson.

Many horses have died in wars. In the Boer War the British alone lost 400,346 horses, donkeys and mules, and in the 1914–18 war many more. The last cavalry charge of history was probably made in World War II by the crack Polish cavalry, who were all but wiped out by the German army.

In peacetime, travel by horse, was the fastest way of getting from one place to another and virtually the only means of transport on land. Ladies rode small horses which could amble, called palfreys. They sat astride or sometimes sideways behind their menfolk. Later horsedrawn carriages of all descriptions were introduced.

Left: The tragic charge of the Light Brigade in the Crimean War is described in Lord Tennyson's famous poem:
'Cannon to right of them,
Cannon to left of them,
Cannon in front of them
Volley'd and thunder'd;
Stormed at with shot and shell
Boldly they rode and well.
Into the jaws of death,
Into the mouth of hell
Rode the six hundred.'

American Indians displayed their incredible riding ability in buffalo hunts on the Great Plains of the West.

The first 'postal' services were effectively run with mounted messengers. In 1860 the famous Pony Express began in America. Despite the harsh terrain and hostile Indians, its riders covered the 3,210 km from Missouri to San Francisco in ten days.

Horse racing had already started in the 17th century, and hunting became a popular sport of the rich.

Horses in the Modern World

With the arrival of the motor car in the 1900s it seemed that the usefulness of horses was at an end. But riding refused to die, and nowadays, all over the world, horses are kept for pleasure as well as work. Societies have grown up to protect them, and riding clubs have mushroomed. Tack has been developed for specific uses, and horses specially bred for different sports.

As well as providing transport, horses are themselves often transported today by air, sea and land to compete all over the world. Television has brought show jumping, cross country events and racing into people's homes. No longer is riding a sport which only the rich can afford. These changes are not always for the good, however, for though horses are now rarely overworked, some stand unridden for months, neglected and bored.

The working horse has not quite vanished. Police horses are still patiently patrolling streets, the best known being the Canadian Mounties in their distinctive uniform. There are film-star horses and many still working with cattle and sheep in Australia and North and South America. Others, such as the horses of the Household Cavalry or the mounted Hussars, are used on ceremonial occasions. They are seen in most of the great capitals of the world, their riders in splendid uniforms escorting kings, queens and presidents, their harnesses jingling, presenting a scene of pageantry at its most colourful.

Finally, the horse can negotiate terrain impossible for a wheeled vehicle, so in spite of modern progress the horse still has a valuable and important role to play in today's technological world.

Performing their ceremonial duties, the Queen's Life Guards provide a colourful spectacle and an example of the perfect partnership between horse and rider.

Saddles for a wide range of purposes have evolved over the centuries.

Learning to Ride

There is really no such thing as a natural rider. Everyone needs lessons, and the best way to learn is at an approved riding school. The choice should exclude a school where the horses are thin and listless. A good school is a happy place with contented horses and clean, well-fitted tack. Most schools can provide a hard hat, but it is better to buy one's own. A safety harness will keep it in place, but should only be worn with a flexible peak; otherwise an elastic under the chin will do. An anorak or warm jersey can be worn, with jeans, though jodhpurs are more comfortable. Sensible shoes or riding boots are a must. Trainers, sandals and plimsolls can slip through stirrups, and high heels and ridged soles can stick in stirrups, causing a nasty accident. In winter or wet weather gloves will be needed, the string or leather type the most suitable. A whip should not be necessary for first lessons.

Left: A riding school with well turned-out horses and a happy atmosphere.

Right: A young rider makes friends with her pony.

Before mounting, the rider should first make friends with his horse or pony, but should not give him titbits without finding out whether the riding school permits it; some schools have strict rules about this. Patting the horse's neck and asking his name is all that is needed. The rider should then check over his tack, making sure, for instance, that the bit is not dangling between his teeth, or the browband over one eye. The next step is to pull up the girths, which are under the large flap and hold the saddle on, and to run down the stirrups, which should have had the leathers tucked into the irons. For a quick measurement of the stirrup length, the fingertips can be placed on the spot where the leathers join the saddle; if the irons reach the armpit they are roughly right; if not, they can be adjusted accordingly. The rider is now ready to mount.

Mounting and Dismounting

When ready to mount, the rider stands on the near (left) side of the horse facing the tail. He then takes the reins in the left hand and separates them with the two middle fingers, letting any loose rein hang over the far side of the horse's neck. He should have enough feel on the reins to stop the horse moving off before he has mounted.

He then takes the stirrup leather in the right hand, turning it so that the smooth side faces him, and puts his left foot in the stirrup iron taking care not to dig it into the horse's side. He then puts his right hand on the pommel or waist of the saddle, springs lightly from the ground, swings his right leg over the saddle and sits down gently. The right foot is then slipped into the offside (right-side) stirrup, twisting the

MOUNTING

1

2

leather so that it lies flat against the leg. The rider is now mounted.

If the horse is big for the rider, a mounting block can be used; this is far better for both the horse and saddle than hauling oneself up by the pommel or cantle. If the horse is difficult to mount, the rider is probably sticking his toe into its stomach. If it tries to walk off before the rider is on, the feel on the reins should be tightened.

Dismounting is far easier. The horse is simply brought to a halt and the rider takes both feet out of the stirrups and puts the reins in the left hand. He then places the right hand on the horse's neck or shoulder to steady himself, leans forward a little, swings his right leg back and over the saddle and slides to the ground. After running up the stirrups the horse can then be led to his stable.

DISMOUNTING

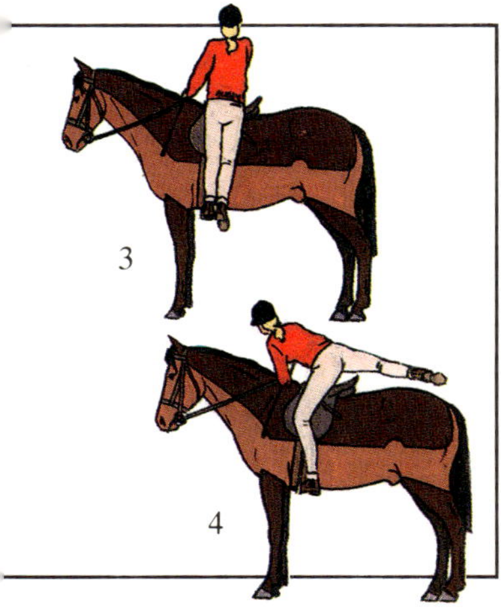

A good seat and leg position are the basis of good riding.

The Seat and Hands

After mounting, the stirrups must be adjusted. For ordinary riding the bottom of the stirrup iron should reach just below the ankle joint when the rider is sitting in the centre of the saddle with his legs hanging down. For jumping, the stirrups must be shorter; for riding Western, longer. Once the stirrups have been adjusted, the rider should make sure they are under the ball of the feet before lowering the heels. He should then sit as straight and tall as possible in the saddle, but relaxed with the weight of the body in the seat bones, thighs and knees. A straight, vertical line from the shoulders should run through the rider's hips to the heels. A line from the knees should pass through the tips of the toes.

Legs too far back tip the rider's weight too far forward and tell the horse to go faster. Legs too far forward throw the weight too far back, and they will be in the wrong place to give aids (instructions) to the horse.

The hands should be steady but relaxed, the wrists flexible but not bent. The reins should pass from the horse's mouth either inside or outside the little finger and under the thumb, which should rest lightly on top, and be held just above the withers with about ten centimetres between them. The hands should be able to act together or independently but should never be used as an anchor to stay on the horse. Double reins should never be used by beginners.

Holding the reins

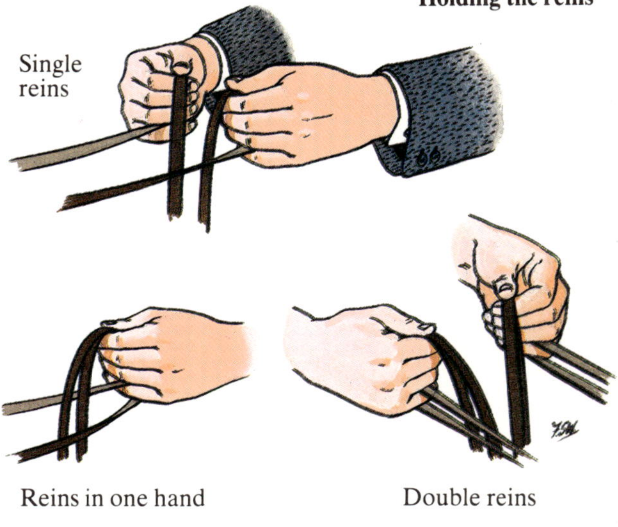

The Aids

The 'natural aids' used to give instructions to the horse are the hands, legs, body and voice. The hands direct the horse through the reins, guiding and controlling pace and forehand (front part). The rider's legs create impulsion and tell the horse to go; they also control the hind quarters. The rider's body is used mainly through the seat. Leaning forward can be an aid to increase speed, while stiffening the spine and sitting down into the saddle will help the hands and legs if the rider wishes to slow down. The voice is important, but should be used sparingly: shouting and screaming is the sign of a bad rider.

The 'artificial aids' are whips, spurs and martingales. A whip should only be used after the rider has given a leg aid and it has been ignored. Martingales are for badly schooled horses, spurs only for the experienced rider.

To move off, the rider relaxes his hands and presses with his legs. To halt, he stiffens his back and tightens the reins, at the same time closing his legs gently against the horse's sides. When the horse halts, the rider relaxes his legs and hands. To turn right, the rider pulls the right rein gently and presses

The artificial aids

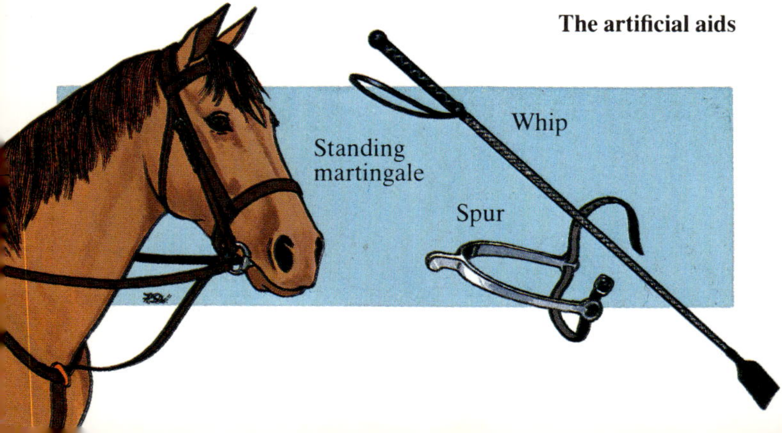

Turning right – although the pony does not look too happy.

with the left leg behind the girth and the right leg on the girth. To turn left, the aids are reversed.

For circling, it is important that the horse should bend his back and neck. For a circle to the left, the left leg is pressed on the girth and the right behind the girth. A light pull is made on the left rein, and the right rein is slackened to enable the horse to bend his neck. Except in circling, the aids should be stopped once the horse has obeyed.

The Paces

THE WALK

The walk is in four-time, which means that a horse moves each leg separately and, if walking on hard ground, makes four distinct hoof-beats. A good walker will pass his front hoof marks with his hind hoof marks. But a horse cannot walk fast on a tight rein: he needs to extend his neck. Jogging is usually caused by too tight a rein. To make the horse walk faster, the rider should use each leg in turn in time with the horse's stride.

The trot is in two-time, which means that the horse moves the legs diagonally in pairs, the near-fore and

THE TROT

off-hind together and the off-fore with the near-hind. When the rider is able to post, or rise off the saddle, at the trot, he should 'change the diagonal' quite often so that he does not always rise or sit to the same pair of legs. A horse raises his head when he trots, so the rider must shorten the reins before pushing him with both legs together. Because the ride is so bumpy, it is important to post. This should be tried first at a walk, simply standing in the stirrups and then sitting down again with the legs in the correct position. The same thing should then be done at a trot in time with the horse's stride. To slow to a walk the rider should stop posting and close his hands on the reins.

THE CANTER

A canter can be as slow as a walk or almost as fast as a gallop. To canter from a trot, the rider must stop posting. If on the straight, he should sit deep in the saddle and push with both legs, keeping only light contact with the reins. When about to turn, circle or ride round a school, the horse must lead on the inside foreleg or he may cross his legs and fall. If riding to the left, this will be the near leg, and the rider must 'feel' (pull gently) on the left rein and press with his left leg on the girth and his right behind it. The aids are reversed for leading on the off leg. If the horse strikes off on the wrong leg, the rider should return to a trot and try again.

At an ordinary canter the rider should sit upright,

comfortable and relaxed, with his legs in the correct place and with the lightest of feel on the horse's mouth. But if riding fast across country or jumping, the stirrups must be shorter and the weight farther forward because, as the horse increases speed to a gallop, he stretches his neck and his body becomes longer and lower. To stay with him the rider must shorten the reins and lean forward. Plenty of space must be allowed for a gallop because the horse may be travelling quite fast and need time to stop. If the rider is inexperienced, he should try galloping uphill first.

The gallop should not be done on hard or muddy ground or on an unfit or recently fed horse.

THE GALLOP

Controlling a Difficult Horse

An inexperienced rider should not be asked to ride a difficult horse. Horses, like other animals, are unpredictable and can have moods. The fault, however, may be the rider's. If the horse is pulling, the leg positions should be checked as they may be too far back and actually telling the horse to go faster. Or the rider may be flourishing a whip, which the horse can see out of the corner of his eye. If not, a long trot, preferably uphill, will settle most troublesome horses. If the horse will not stop when galloping, he should be turned in ever decreasing circles until he stops. If he will not move, it is often because he wants to stay with other horses, and a whip to back up a leg aid should be effective.

A rearing horse

Bits in common use

Eggbutt jointed snaffle

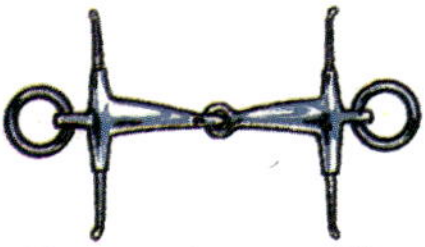

Loose ring snaffle

Mullen mouth snaffle

Weymouth and Bridoon

Pelham

Bronco riding at an American rodeo illustrates a novel way of staying on.

But the rider should check that the cause is not lameness or ill-fitting tack.

Dismounting and going first will often coax a nervous horse past a terrifying object, but this should not become a habit. A horse which constantly rears is not safe to ride because he may fall back on to the rider. Bucking horses usually do so through high spirits or to dislodge the rider. More exercise will cure the first; schooling him and being a better rider should stop the second. A change of bit sometimes helps to control a difficult horse, but often only temporarily. Martingales assist in keeping the horse's head in the correct place, and a running one gives the rider more leverage. But well-schooled horses need neither martingales nor complex bits. Re-training is the real answer to most difficult horses. The exception is, of course, the rodeo horse, who bucks for his living.

Jumping

The rider should begin jumping by trotting over a heavy pole on the ground, looking straight ahead. Another pole can then be added, and then another, with about 120 cm between each depending on the size of the horse and the length of his stride. When the rider can do this quietly and confidently he should pull the stirrups up one or two holes and practise a jumping seat. This involves leaning forward to take the weight off the horse's quarters, letting the hands go forward so that he can stretch his neck freely, and keeping the heels down with the weight in the knees. A good jumping seat is hard to achieve, but the rider must persist.

A small cavaletto can now be placed about 2.5 metres from the last pole and ridden over. Just before the horse takes off, the rider may grab the mane or neckstrap until he feels safe, but must never hold on by the reins. He can then continue jumping from a trot, adding more fences but keeping them low until he can jump without losing his seat. He can then try jumping from a canter, making sure the horse is going steadily before beginning. If the horse starts to rush, the rider should turn him away from the fence and try again when he is calmer. Approaching the fence, the hands should be near the

Above: A rider keeps a good seat from take-off to landing.

Below: A young rider clears a natural fence comfortably.

withers and, as the horse jumps, go forward with him as he stretches his neck. As he lands, the rider must regain his seat and keep the horse balanced for the next fence, without looking back to see whether the fence has fallen.

It is important for the rider to jump in a school or an enclosed space until he is confident he has full control of the horse. Good riders ride quietly, without flapping their legs wildly or pulling the reins violently.

Some Common Faults

When the horse stops in front of or on the approach to a fence and will not go over, this is called 'refusing'. The fence may be too high for him; he may be sour from too much jumping; the rider may be nervous or may have jerked his mouth; or he may even be reluctant to leave other horse friends. The cause should be sought and remedied. If the rider has been jumping the horse a great deal, he should hack instead; if the rider is nervous, he should wait until he is feeling braver; and he should lean forward earlier to stop jerking the horse's mouth. Constant jumping over high fences tends to sour even the best horses; it is far better to school over interesting combinations and a constantly changing, quite low course.

A good jump, except that the rider is looking down and her legs are too far back.

A sudden stop as the pony refuses a fence, but the rider is still in control.

Avoiding a jump by 'running out' to the side can be caused by too long a run, or a very narrow fence. Most horses always run out one way, so the rider should try a shorter run and ride towards the other end of the fence; the horse should then arrive in the middle and go over. But running out really means the horse needs more schooling and a better rider.

If the horse suddenly stops jumping completely, it may be because he has aching legs or has a painful back. With an old horse, the cause may be the onset of some disease, such as navicular, ringbone or arthritis. Developing splints or spavins will have the same effect on a younger horse. If this seems likely, the horse should be examined by a vet.

Finally, jumping should never be attempted on hard or slippery ground or just after the horse has been fed and watered. Remembering to reward the horse when he has done well is also important.

Fences and Courses

All kinds of simple fences can be built from a wide range of materials. A wall can be made, for instance, from an old door painted to resemble bricks, and other simple fences devised provided they look solid and are not flimsy. Except for logs, fences should fall down when knocked hard but not blow down in the wind. No fence should be less than three metres long, unless 'wings' are used at each end. The poles should be heavy, the supports solid and movable. These can include oil drums or straw bales. Whatever the fence, it should not have a lot of daylight under it. An ideal school fence is the cavaletto, a pole between two crossed-shaped supports. Spread fences, such as triples, hogs' backs and doubles, are also excellent for schooling, because they all have a lower rail which helps a horse to take off in the right place.

Building a course is not easy, and most shows employ a specialist to do it. Combination fences are particularly difficult, as the distances between each one must be right and because a pony will need less room than a horse. In a combination the widest fence should be used as the last spread; a triple should never be put first or before two upright fences. A gate should never lean towards a rider as this creates a false ground line and is an impossible fence for all but the most experienced horses.

To build a really professional course, it is best to obtain a book containing diagrams from a horse society or club. In this way a safe course can be built and changed frequently to provide greater interest and better training for both rider and horse.

Simple fences

Log

Straw bales

Tyres

Oil drums

Pole with ground line

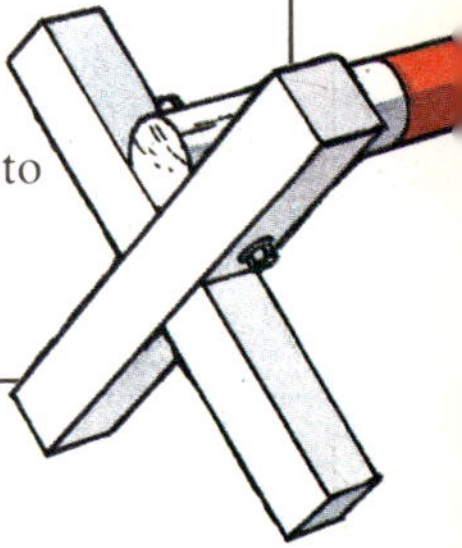

Cavaletto

Hacking Out

Riding along busy roads is dangerous, particularly when alone. When in a crowd, riders should proceed in single file, unless there is a nervous horse in the group, when it helps to place a steady horse between it and the traffic. Riders should signal when turning, and thank, either with the hand or vocally, those drivers who slow down for them. Riders should never race along roads, particularly at a canter, as this is not only highly dangerous but also bad for the horse's legs. A nervous horse should not be forced past a frightening object until the road is clear; the traffic should be stopped if necessary, because riders

Riding in single file along a country road, with a safe distance between each horse.

Good riders always give clear signals of their intentions or wishes.

have the right of way. However, they should never ride off the roadside verge without looking behind first, and in a town they should observe traffic lights and keep off the sidewalk. If riding at dawn or dusk, fluorescent clothing and/or stirrup lights should be worn. It is always advisable to be properly insured against accident through the Pony Club or a riding club or some other scheme.

Hacking through the countryside can be a pleasant experience, but riders should watch for rabbit holes and low tree branches. Someone should be told where the rider plans to go so that if he falls off he can be found. By walking quietly out of the yard and over the last kilometre back home, the horse can be brought in cool. The length and speed of the ride should be built up gradually to give the horse time to get fit before setting out on a marathon.

Care of the Countryside

All over the world riders use known and well-worn tracks through the countryside. In some countries, many of these tracks have been in existence for hundreds of years, like the bridleways of Britain. Most of these, though they may cross private land, are part of the national heritage and belong to everyone. But whether passing through private or public land, riders should always behave with consideration for others and care for the countryside. Throwing rubbish down, splashing walkers with mud, shouting and screaming, all give riding a bad name. High spirits should not be allowed to ruin the countryside for everyone else. Riders must keep to the proper tracks, with their horses under control at all times, and slow down for the young, the old and the lame, and for any animal they may meet.

Left: Stay right at the edge of any field under cultivation.

Above: Closing a gate correctly, with the horse's tail to the hinges.

Do's and Don'ts When Riding in the Country

Don't ride over growing crops.
Don't gallop near sheep or cattle.
Don't throw down lighted matches.
Don't lark over fences without permission.
Don't build jumps on private property.
Do shut gates.
Do ride quietly through farmyards and past children.
Do be polite to people you meet. A 'good morning' will earn a good mark for all riders.
Do go quietly past other riders, particularly beginners, or you may start a stampede.

Trekking

Riders enjoying an orderly trek through wild countryside.

Riding over long distances through the countryside, or trekking, is a popular sport worldwide and is enjoyed by thousands every year who would never otherwise have a chance to ride. Most trekking centres are near mountains and provide accommodation which can be simply tents or sumptuously equipped rooms with private baths; most are between these extremes. If preferred, riders may of course arrange their own accommodation elsewhere.

Anyone can trek, because rides vary in speed and length to suit every rider. The horses vary from quite small ponies to those of hunter size, but most are between 13.2 and 15.2 hands. Warm, waterproof clothing is often needed, as well as good boots, but most centres provide hats. Sometimes the rider is allotted a horse for his stay and is expected to look after it, and in this way he learns some stable management also.

Riding and Pony Clubs

There are nearly 2,000 branches of the Pony Club with a total membership in 1981 of around 126,838, Australia alone having 669 branches and a membership of 35,450 and Britain 47,358 members. But it is not only in the Western Hemisphere that the Pony Club flourishes; there are around 3,997 members in Japan, others in Saudi Arabia, Singapore, Botswana, the United States, Canada, Thailand, New Zealand -- far too many to list here. Membership is for anyone under 21 years (you do not need a horse of your own). There are also riding clubs throughout the world for older riders. Addresses can be obtained from the Pony Club or British Horse Society, The National Equestrian Centre, Kenilworth, Warwickshire, England, if they cannot be found nearer to home.

The end of a competition at a Pony Club camp.

A jumping lesson in progress at a Pony Club camp.

The working rally is the most important fixture of the Pony Club, for it is here members receive expert help and instruction free. This covers stable management and all aspects of horsemanship as well as riding, and members failing to attend these fixtures are disqualified from Club events and eventually lose their membership. Other fixtures include lectures, film shows, treasure and mock hunts, children's meets and long distance rides. Inter-branch competitions foster pride in individual branches and offer a chance to meet other members. The best known, the Mounted Games (the Prince Philip Cup), culminates in Britain at Wembley in October. There are also area quizzes, a polo tournament, show jumping, and the horse trial championships, with competitions varying slightly from country to country. More and more teams are travelling abroad to compete against one another.

Negotiating a cross country fence at a Pony Club camp.

In many Pony Clubs, camp is the highlight of the year. Conditions vary, with tented accommodation in some, huts or barns in others. In all, it is fairly spartan, which adds to the fun. Horses are turned out with hind shoes removed to avoid injury to one another, or stood in lines, or in stalls or loose boxes. Days begin with mucking out and feeding, followed by a hearty breakfast. Instruction follows grooming and tacking up, with help for those about to take tests or ride in teams. In the afternoon there are often lectures and demonstrations on general horsemanship. In the evening there may be more riding, perhaps a rehearsal for a musical ride or a hack out. Visits to places of interest and test days are often included. Most camps end with a display, horse show or gymkhana, perhaps all three. A Jumping with Dressage competition is often held for the older members.

A young Pony Club rider admires her rosette. Rosettes are awarded for various other activities as well as riding at the Pony Club camp.

Rosette

Tests are an important part of the Pony Club and range from test D at the bottom, through C, B, H, and A (H is primarily concerned with the care of horses). All members are expected to try for these certificates, which are useful evidence of the standard reached. There are also scholarship courses arranged to assist instructors, and competent horsemen or women are always welcome to help in this capacity. Assistance is needed too with clerical work and for camp cooking.

Riding clubs are run on much the same lines and most organize their own events and give help and instruction where needed. Many give displays ranging from dressing as Canterbury pilgrims, to performing a quadrille. They also compete in teams, and some shows run a special class for riding clubs. To join you usually must be over 17.

Competitions and Sport

Competitive riding has grown tremendously over the years and has changed dramatically since slats were placed on fences claiming half a fault each time they were displaced. In those days courses consisted of six fences, five round the outside and a triple in the middle. Few could have dreamed that horse shows would be held all over the world and that the great show jumpers, equine and human, would become household names, that members of the British royal family would be competing in cross country events and that riding would become a sport enjoyed by millions. Yet most of the great riders of today started in quite a small way at local gymkhanas and Pony Club rallies on small ponies, or in the hunting field.

A class in progress at a typical horse show.

Dressage

A rider in the dressage arena.

A dressage test is a test of a horse's training; it takes place in a small arena within a certain time. A heavy, badly made horse is unlikely to be successful at dressage for, though he may become accurate with schooling, he will never have the carriage and action for all but the most elementary of tests. Temperament is important too, because a tense rider or an excitable horse cannot accomplish a good test, which must be graceful and unhurried. A dressage test should be learned before it is ridden but only by the rider not the horse, who will tend to anticipate every movement if he knows it in advance. Bearing this in mind, it is best to ride the test in sections rather than the whole of it together. Good hands and seat are needed for dressage, and it is pointless to compete in a test before a reasonable standard of riding has been reached.

Show Jumping

Most people have watched show jumping on television. The great riders of the world, performing flawlessly over enormous fences, make it look easy. But it has taken years of work and dedication to reach such a standard. And now that show jumping tends to last all the year round toughness and stamina are necessary too, as well as the brains to cope with the enormous, complicated courses of today.

Courses are carefully constructed and planned to suit the horses taking part, with stiles, walls, gates,

A rider races against the clock in an exciting jump-off.

brushes, double oxers, triple bars, planks, hogs' backs, crossed bars, road closed fences and water jumps. All must be placed with the right distance between them, and the combinations carefully measured to give a horse a fair chance to clear them safely. Three fences with less than 12 metres between each become a combination, two a double.

In affiliated shows jumpers must be registered. They are graded and a tally of their wins kept. In this way experienced horses cannot compete against novices. As well as the more usual events, there are timed ones such as Take Your Own Line, Scurry and Pair Relay, in which time may be added rather than jumping faults, that is, 6–10 seconds added for each fence knocked down. Hit and Hurry, Have a Gamble and Accumulator also have their own rules. Elsewhere the standard faults apply: 4 faults for a knock down, 3 for a first refusal, 6 for a second (making 9), elimination for a third, fall of horse and rider or rider alone, 8 faults. Starting before the bell and leaving the ring out of control brings elimination. Circling before a fence once the bell has rung also counts as a refusal, and taking the wrong course means elimination.

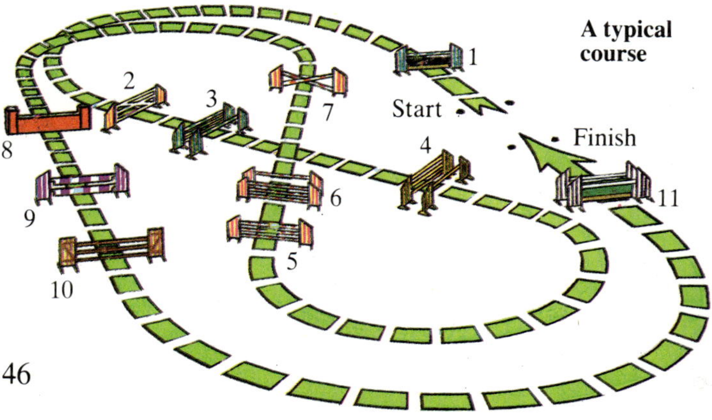

A typical course

A fantastic leap takes a rider safely over the water jump.

A rider who wishes to take up show jumping should start at small local shows. Success will largely depend on him, because even the best show jumpers will not go on winning with an incompetent rider. Having entered before the show, the rider should walk the course before competing, not only because he must know it but also because he needs to plan how to ride each fence, remembering that spreads and water need speed, and uprights a steadier approach. Corners must be cut in a timed jump-off, and sometimes it is a gamble whether to cut one and risk knocking a fence, or take the long way round and lose seconds. A young or inexperienced horse, however, should never be overtaxed, because if his nerve is destroyed he may never show-jump again. Four-year-olds should not be raced against the clock, and even six or seven is still young for a show jumper; many of the international stars are much older.

An elegant young rider presents a well turned-out pony at a show.

Showing

There are classes for every type of horse and pony. In working or green hunter classes, horses are expected to jump a course of natural fences before being judged on conformation. In family pony classes an animal must prove itself really quiet, and suitable for all the family to ride. A first pony must be absolutely safe. As for the others, it is often a matter of training, fitness and conformation, turn-out, and, except in 'in hand' classes, accomplished riding. Showing is an art to be learned, and copying expert riders is a good way of achieving it. The rider's clothes must be suitable: a riding hat, dark coat, boots, clean jodhpurs or breeches, gloves and a neat cane or riding stick; the hair must be short and tidy or in a net, and the tack clean. A show saddle helps, as do plaits, and a double bridle in some hunter classes.

When the competitor is actually in the ring he must keep his distance from other riders: to be on his own and visible is all-important. When called in, he should enter the line-up from the back and keep the horse standing straight and on the bit, not resting a leg or grazing. If it is necessary to remove the saddle, the competitor should have someone ready with brush or rubber to remove sweat marks. He should trot out with the reins over the horse's head, pushing him away when turning. If the judge is riding, the competitor should be sure the girths are tight and should help him mount. When asked to give a 'show', the competitor should make it neat, effective and not too long, remembering that in family pony classes he must show the pony's reliability even if it means sliding over tails, carrying stuffed sacks or something equally unusual.

A line-up of winners in a child's first pony class.

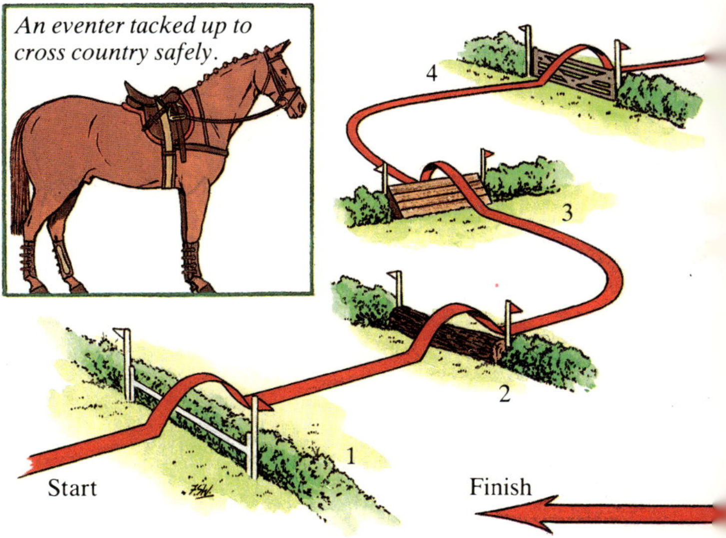

An eventer tacked up to cross country safely.

Cross Country Events

First named 'The Military', then 'Combined Training', early cross country competitions were designed to test the fitness of horse and rider for military service. Now called horse trials or eventing, our modern versions begin with a dressage phase to test obedience, followed by a course to be negotiated of perhaps 27 kilometres combining a section of roads and tracks, a steeplechase course and a cross country course of 7 kilometres with a host of formidable fences. And finally, the next day a course of painted fences must be jumped to prove that the horse is still sound. This is a full-blooded three-day event held all over the world and an Olympic event. The most famous is held every spring at Badminton in Gloucestershire, England.

There are also less arduous events. A one-day

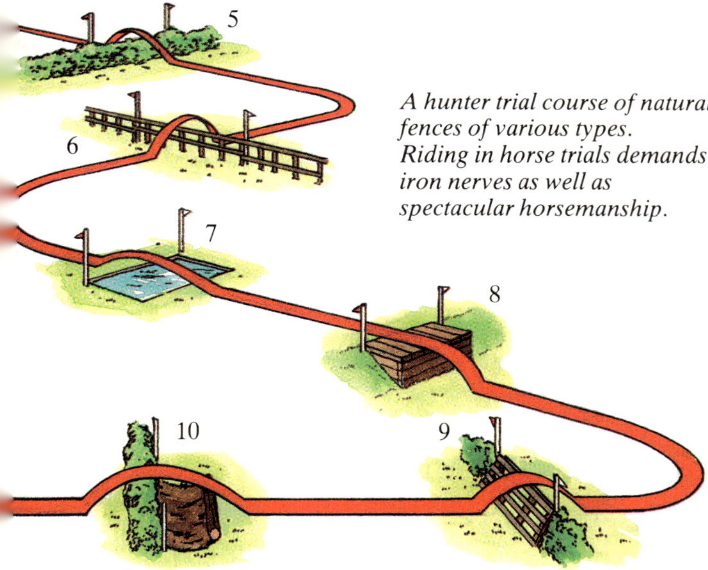

A hunter trial course of natural fences of various types. Riding in horse trials demands iron nerves as well as spectacular horsemanship.

event is likely to be easier, so are small local ones, some being held for riders as young as ten or eleven. These are all good schooling grounds, but for the really big events the rider must qualify, and this means winning or being placed in recognized competitions.

Today's eventer needs great courage, stamina, talent and an enormously high standard of fitness if he is to succeed. Nothing is crueller than asking an unfit horse to compete in horse trials; it is far better to concentrate on the easier hunter trials, which are run mainly by hunts over natural fences. Judging may be on style, or on speed, or by bogey time. Pair and team events are often included and there are generally children's classes. Some Pony Clubs run their own hunter trials.

Gymkhanas

Reputed to have started in India when the British were there, gymkhanas are excellent competitions for riders and a good schooling ground for ponies if ridden properly. Mounted games are a feature of Pony Club life, each branch usually producing one or more teams. Gymkhanas are mainly for individuals on ordinary ponies. Spurs and whips are banned in competitions, and a good pony temperament and an agile rider are needed. Most successful competitors have worked hard over many weeks and it is this rather than an expensive pony which produces a champion.

It is best to start practising at a trot before competing at faster paces. Good slow ground work is better than a lot of galloping. The rider should try riding in one hand, teaching the pony to stop when

An exciting start to a sack race.

Some gymkhana events

Sack race

Apple and bucket race

Musical poles

Potato race

he says 'Whoa', and to gallop from a standstill.

There are enough gymkhana events to suit most ponies and riders. The 'ride and run' obviously needs a fast runner and a pony that leads well. The potato race requires a good aim, the carton race a steady hand. Musical poles or sacks needs the competitor's concentration to make sure he is in a good place when the music stops and that he knows where he is going. Apple bobbing and the sack race can be practised at home without the pony.

The competitor should try to do everything as calmly and smoothly as possible. He should never shout at his pony or make a fuss about losing. He must also be certain he knows the rules before entering the ring, because they are not always the same. Some organizers even make them up as they go along.

Long Distance and Trail Riding

There is no distinction between trail and long distance riding and no world organization to co-ordinate the sport. The most famous ride in the United States is the Western States Trail Ride for the Tevis Cup. Covering 160 kilometres, it takes riders along the original Indian route from the Californian gold mines to Nevada. In Australia riders have to qualify for the Tom Quilty Endurance rides, and no whips or spurs are allowed. Over the 173 kilometres, horses must carry 72·5 kilogrammes in weight. In South Africa the National Endurance Ride is 210 kilometres long and is covered in three days.

Above: A keen competitor in a long distance ride.

In Britain the Arab Society holds its annual Marathon in October, and the Golden Horse Shoe Ride across Exmoor is now well known.

Rules and judging vary tremendously. In Britain rides are sometimes divided into ordinary and fast; the first must clock up an average speed of 9–11 kmh, the second 13–14 kmh. Marked deviations from these speeds are penalized. In South Africa an award is made to the horse in the best condition among the first ten to finish. In some rides competitors have to carry food for both themselves and their horses. These rides call for a really fit horse, and training must be long and thorough. It is interesting that so many have been won by Arabs or by Australian stock horses possibly with Arab origins.

Below: Rugged country in Idaho, as in other parts of the American West, offers spectacular scenery for trail riders.

Polo

Originating in Iran and northern India, polo is an international game, and the best grounds are probably to be found in the United States and South America. Lasting 60 minutes, a game is divided into eight periods called chukkas, and there are four players a side. The height limit for ponies was abolished after the First World War and they can now be of any size, and many a champion has come from Argentina. Because a player needs several ponies, polo tends to be a rich man's game. However, helped by the Pony Club and its popularity with Prince Charles, the game is making a comeback in Britain and is now played throughout the season at Smith's Lawn, Windsor. The Pony Club holds an annual tournament and, although a top pony may cost large sums, most ponies can be trained to play a slow game.

The action is fast and furious in a polo chukka.

Hunting

A huntsman and his whipper-in with hounds.

Hunting goes back thousands of years, but it was not until the 18th century that packs were used to hunt specific animals. The speed of a run depends almost as much on terrain as the quarry hunted. In Virginia, in the United States, jumps, mainly of timber, are taken at great speed. In France the wild boar is hunted, mostly through forests. In Britain barbed wire and motorways have spoilt much hunting country and although in the shires fast runs are still common, in mountainous regions the story is different. Drag hunting is growing in popularity and also hunting with bloodhounds. Supporters clubs are patronised by both car and foot followers. A hunt staff consists of a huntsman and usually two whippers-in. The master may hunt hounds or control the field (followers).

Racing

The racing colours worn by jockeys identify the horses' owners.

Racing in Britain consists of flat racing and steeplechasing, and since the 17th century its centre has been Newmarket. The Derby, founded in 1780, is probably the most famous race of all, and not only in Britain, for Calcutta in India has its own Derby, and Kenya has the Nairobi Derby run in January. And in the United States there is no more famous race than the Kentucky Derby. Among other races, the Melbourne Cup is a classic founded in 1831, and there are many classic races held in France.

Steeplechasing began in 1752 with that renowned race run in Ireland for a bet from one church steeple to another over 7·2 kilometres. Run over the same

Jockeys ride with short stirrups.

distance and with 30 fences, the celebrated Grand National, held at Aintree near Liverpool, is today the longest steeplechase in the world, closely followed by the Grand Pardubice in Czechoslovakia, which in 1937 was won by a woman.

In Britain racehorses often start their careers as yearlings and are considered old horses at four years. Australian racehorses are broken at 18 months. To be a jockey is the ambition of many a youngster, though the life is hard and the knocks frequent. But if he can make the grade the rewards are many: adulation, fame, and the thrill of having millions of pounds or dollars worth of horse between the knees. A jockey is never far away from horses, and nothing surpasses the sensation of coming into the last furlong first, with the roar of the crowd in one's ears. If a rider wants to be a steeplechase jockey, riding at point-to-points is the best way to begin. Run mainly by hunts, the pace is slower and the fences less formidable than in the top steeplechases.

Racing at Epsom, England.

Some Famous Horses and Riders

Copenhagen, the Duke of Wellington's chestnut stallion, was ridden nearly 100 km before the battle of Waterloo without a break. The next day he was on the battlefield for 17 hours. Retired to Berkshire, he died in 1836 and was buried with full military honours.

Inciatus, a Roman racehorse, must have been famous in his day, for he was appointed a Senator by his mad master, the emperor Caligula.

Marengo, Napoleon's beloved grey stallion, was ridden through many a long campaign and at the battle of Waterloo. His skeleton is at the National Army Museum, England.

Morocco was a famous 17th-century performing horse that could count numbers turned up by dice with his hoof. In Italy his tricks were dubbed black magic and he and his owner Thomas Bankes were condemned to death by burning. Bankes escaped but Morocco's fate is unknown.

Red Rum, foaled in 1965, and bought for only £420 as a four-year-old, went on to win the Grand National steeplechase more times than any other horse.

Paul Revere, an American silversmith, signalled the start of the War of Independence with his famous ride from Boston to

Lexington, Massachusetts, to warn of an imminent attack by British forces.

Grabeik Stecher rode his horse Arab Sahlawi bareback through the entire Tom Quilty Endurance Ride in 1966 and won it in 11 hours 24 minutes.

Aime Felix Tschiffely rode 16,000 km from Buenos Aires to Washington D.C. in 1925 to prove the stamina of Criollo horses. Riding on Mancha, aged 16 years, and Gato, a year younger, he took 2½ years and suffered great hardship. Mancha died aged 40 and Gato at 36, surely proving the stamina of their breed.

Wellington on Copenhagen.

Napoleon on Marengo.

Paul Revere dashes through the night on his famous ride in April 1775 to warn the American patriots of a British attack.

Index

Acknowledgements
The author and publishers gratefully acknowledge the assistance of the following in supplying the photographs on the pages indicated:
Animal Photography Ltd. 25
Fotomas Index 10, 11
Kit Houghton *frontispiece*, 54 (top), 57
Mansell Collection 60, 61
Peter Newark's Western Americana 27, 54–55 (bottom)
Peter Roberts 14, 15, 16, 17, 21, 22, 23, 24, 30, 31, 32, 34, 37, 42, 43, 44, 45, 47, 48, 49, 52, 56
Sally Anne Thompson 29, 38, 39, 40, 41, 59
ZEFA/ V. Wentzel 9

Thanks are also expressed to the Belmont Country Club & Equestrian Centre, London, and Frith Manor Livery Stables, London.